The Book of Horses

THIS IS A MORTIMER CHILDREN'S BOOK

Published in 2019 by Mortimer Children's
an imprint of the Welbeck Publishing Group
20 Mortimer Street, London W1T 3JW

Text, design, and illustration © Welbeck Publishing Limited 2019

ISBN: 978 1 78312 515 9

Designed, written, and packaged by: Dynamo Limited
Art editor: Deborah Vickers
Editor: Jenni Lazell
Production: Nicola Davey

The publishers would like to thank the following sources for their
kind permission to reproduce the pictures in this book. Every effort has been
made to acknowledge correctly and contact the source and/or copyright holder
of each picture. Any unintentional errors or omissions will be corrected in
future editions of this book.

T = Top; L = Left; C = Center; R = Right; b = Bottom

Alamy: /BSIP SA: 27BR; /Alexander Frolov: 27C; /Paul Hawkett: 35C; /Interfoto: 40BL; /Juniors Bildarchiv GmbH: 63BR, 67BL, 67BR; /Bob Langrish: 62BL, 69TR; /Doug Steley A: 26TR; **Shutterstock:** /3DMI: 24B (grass); /Abramova Kseniya: 31; /Ad van Brunschot: 26B (dandy brush); /Alexia Khruscheva: 10TR, 11TC; /Alicia Marvin: 66TR; /anakondasp: 26B (body brush & plastic curry comb); /Andrea Izzotti: 69TL; /anjajuli: 23BL; /ANL: 47TR; /anyamay: 40R; /AP: 47BR; /arthorse: 9R, 12L, 60; /azure1: 25L (nettles); /Bartkowski: 55BL; /bergamont: 25B (tomato); /bigacis: 24B (banana); /Bosnian: 67TR; /Callipso: 4-5, 48TR, 70-71; /Carlos E Santa Maria: 55TR; /Cathleen A Clapper: 26B (metal curry comb); /CD_Photography: 43; /Conny Sjostrom: 8L; /David Wieczorek: 56BL; /Davydenko Yuliia: 25B (chocolate); /Dennis W Donohue: 39; /Diane Garcia: 38; /Edoma: 69BR; /Eric Isselee: 10TC, 23C, 48BL; /Everett Collection: 35BL; /Fotografiecor.nl: 25TR; /Francey: 17BL; /gabriel12: 66BL; /Gerasimov Sergei: 12-13; /GeptaYs: 8-9, 10BR; /gibieho: 34; /Glynnis Jones: 42; /Gpaul photography: 61; /Granger: 41; /gresei: 25B (meat); /Gudkov Andrey: 58-59; /hedgehog94: 22BR; /igorstevanovic: 26B (sponge); /jacotakepics: 11BR; /Juan Aunion: 23BR; /Julia Remezova: 11TL, 11TR; /karengesweinphotography: 28-29; /keerati: 24TR; /Konenko Oleksandr: 2-3; /Kovaleva_Ka: 24B (apple); /Kwadrat: 17R; /Lisa Kolbenschlag: 68TR; /M. Rohana: 36-37; /Makarova Viktoria: 14; /Maks Narodenko: 24B & 25C (mint), 25B (garlic); /mariait: 1, 11BC, 57; /Mavritsina Irina: 63TL; /Meriennah: 13R; /Mick Atkins: 35TR; /Miguel G. Saavedra: 24B (celery); /Mihai Stanciu: 16L; /Moviestore: 46; /Nata-Lia: 25B (onion); /Nattika: 24B (carrot), 25B (potato); /Nicole Ciscato: 56TR, 62TR; /oceanwhisper: 16BR; /Olesya Nakipova: 32; /Olga_i: 10BL, 10BC, 33, 52-53; /olgaru79: 15; /Osetrik: 11BL, 44; /photo-equine: 68L; /Picsoftheday: 21; /picturepartners: 24B & 25TR (cow parsley); /pirita: 30; /Rawpixel.com: 50-51; /rokopix: 49; /RowanArtCreation: 25TC; /Sari ONeal: 68BR; /Shestakoff: 27TL, 27TR; /shoot66: 18-19; /snapvision: 66BR; /Sue Robinson: 25R; /SunnyMoon: 69BL; /sunsinger: 64-65; /Svetlana Ryazantseva: 23TR; /Tamara Didenko: 6-7; /tanya_morozz: 22TR; /timages: 26B (mane comb); /trotalo: 37BR; /Valentine Shepitko: 45; /Vera Zinkova: 54; /Xara Kreta: 47L; /xpixel: 24B & 25B (hay); /Zuzule: 20, 67TL

Printed in Heshan, China

9 8 7 6 5 4 3 2 1

The Book of Horses

The ultimate guide to horses around the world

MORTIMER

Contents

Welcome

Inside this book is everything you need to know about horses. We'll take you through everything from points to polo, and equestrian sports to riding tips. This book is packed with beautiful photographs of wild ponies and rare breeds, as well as an extra cute foal feature. What's more, you'll get the chance to explore the record-breaking horses of the world.

Have you ever wondered what the difference is between a horse and pony? Now you can find out once and for all.

What is a horse?

These beautiful creatures are part of the Equidae family and come in many different breeds, colors, and sizes.

Intelligent, loyal, and gentle, horses have helped humans in many different ways throughout history. From farming to mining, in the police force and as therapy—it's no wonder they are loved around the world.

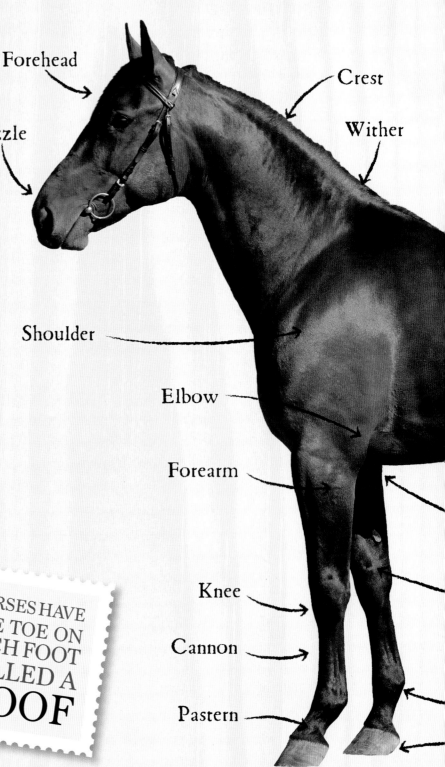

Forehead

Muzzle

Crest

Wither

Shoulder

Elbow

Forearm

Knee

Cannon

Pastern

HORSES HAVE ROUGHLY **205** BONES

HORSES HAVE ONE TOE ON EACH FOOT CALLED A **HOOF**

Measuring

Horses are measured in hands, and each hand is 4 inches long. HH means "hands high." You measure the height of the horse from the ground to its withers (top of its shoulders).

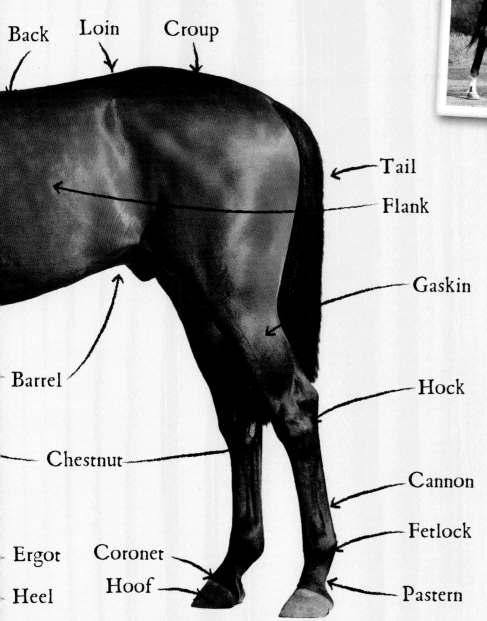

Back

Loin

Croup

Tail

Flank

Gaskin

Barrel

Hock

Chestnut

Cannon

Fetlock

Ergot Coronet

Heel Hoof

Pastern

NOTHINGS GETS PAST A HORSE—THEIR EYES ARE POSITIONED SO THAT **THEY CAN SEE 350 DEGREES**

Did you know?

Horses can snooze, even when they're standing up. It's all because of a unique locking mechanism in their knees.

Coat colors

Horses have lots of different types of coat patterns and horse colorings.

Palomino

Palominos are noticeable for their golden coats and light manes that can range from white to yellow.

Bay

Bays have a brown coat with a black mane, tail, ears, and lower legs. This is a very common color combination.

Gray

There are many varying shades of gray coats. Gray horses usually start out a much darker gray, or even brown, as foals.

Dun

Duns are cream-colored with a black mane and tail. This combination is thought to be the original horse coloring!

Brown

These horses have a dark brown coat with a lighter brown muzzle. They have black lower legs, tail, and mane.

Chestnut

Chestnuts are known for their reddish-brown (chestnut-colored) coats. Unlike Bays, they don't have any black accents.

Black

It is uncommon for horses to be completely black. If their coats don't change color in the sun, they're called "non-fading."

Spotted

This distinctive coat pattern can be in any color. Appaloosas are a breed known for their spotted coats.

Pinto horse

These horses have large patches of white and other colors. The word "paint" is sometimes used to describe their coloring.

Cremello

Although these horses look white, they are actually a very pale cream. They often have blue eyes, too.

Roan

Roans have a mixture of colored and white hairs on their body, while the tail, mane, and legs are solid blocks of color.

Perfect patterns

Now that you know how to identify the various horse colorings, it's time to get to grips with face markings and their names. By the end of these pages, you should know your blaze from your snip, and everything in between.

Face markings

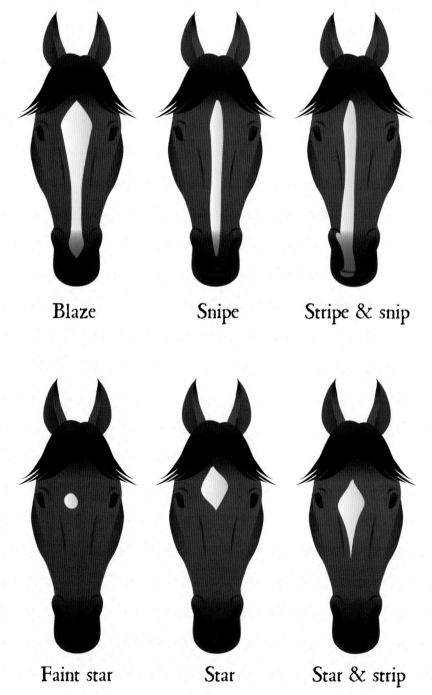

Blaze

Snipe

Stripe & snip

Faint star

Star

Star & strip

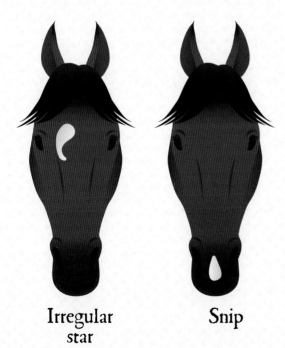

Irregular blaze

Bald face

Irregular
star

Snip

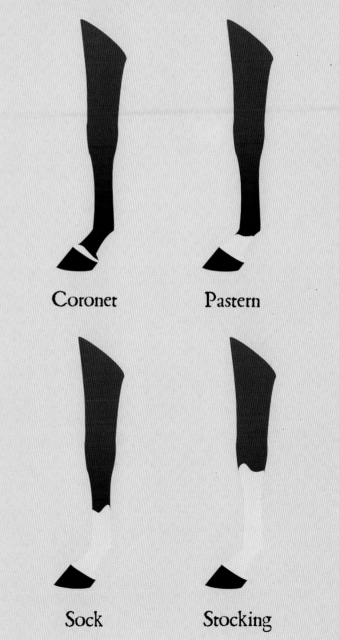

Leg markings

Horses' faces are not the only places where they sport distinctive patterns. Take a look at these interesting leg markings, too.

Coronet

Pastern

Sock

Stocking

Appaloosa

The Palouse River Horse

Instantly recognizable with their spotted coats and striped hooves, Appaloosas were first bred in the American West by the Nez Perce Tribe. They get their name from the Palouse River in Idaho, which was at the heart of Nez Perce territory. This speedy breed often appears in show jumping and competitions, as well as races. Their gentle ways make them an ideal breed for beginners. Plus, they're so loyal, they'll be a friend for life.

Friesian

The Mane Event

This beautiful breed originates in Friesland, in the Netherlands. Their history dates back to the 13th century—making them one of the oldest breeds. The muscular creatures are famous for their glossy, thick mane, and feathered legs. Friesians are placid and willing to learn, and have historically been used for farm work. In fact, there was a fear of them going extinct in the early 20th century due to the invention of machinery for agricultural work. They are not great at jumping events, but Friesians are popular in dressage because they're so elegant.

Did you know?

Although Friesians are usually black, some can be chestnut-colored.

Horses versus ponies

There is a lot of confusion about the difference between a horse and a pony. Some believe that ponies are just baby horses! So, let's set the record straight once and for all.

In common:

> Horses and ponies are the same species— *Equus Caballus*

> They both come from the same family tree

> Lots of ponies and horses compete in dressage and jumping

> Both are measured in hands

Differences

> They have different bone structures and proportions. For example, ponies have shorter legs and a thicker neck

> Ponies live longer than horses—sometimes over 30 years!

> Horses eat more than ponies

> Horses take longer to grow

> For their size, ponies are stronger than horses

> Ponies have thicker coats to protect them—very handy for wild pony breeds

Did you know?

Horses have the largest eyes of all land mammals.

Wild ponies

There are many types of wild pony roaming the countryside, from Welsh Mountain ponies to the Polish Konik. Besides looking beautiful and drawing in tourists, these animals have to be very resilient to live in harsh environments. Find out about another wild breed, the Dartmoor pony, here.

Don't underestimate this pony!

This breed has lived in Dartmoor in England for centuries. They may be small, but the Dartmoor pony is tough enough to cope with extreme conditions on the moors. Food is limited, but this doesn't stop them from thriving. Their grazing plays a vital role in maintaining a variety of habitats and supporting wildlife. Dartmoor ponies wander freely, but they belong to the farmers and residents of the moor. The breed is known to be gentle and calm and comes in a variety of colors. Over the years, this particular breed has been used in mining and shepherding.

No matter how tempting it is, you should never feed wild ponies. It can encourage them to stay around the roads, which is very dangerous. They must stick to their natural diet to avoid getting ill.

Did you know?

Dartmoor ponies are the logo of England's Dartmoor National Park, and are a big tourist attraction.

Budyonny

Originally, Budyonny were developed as a military horse. The breed was named after a cavalry commander named Marshall Semyon Budyonny who became famous following the Russian Revolution. They are long-legged and often chestnut-colored. Budyonny are a strong build of horse—similar to the Thoroughbred breed.

Brumby

Brumby are an Australian free-roaming horse that live in the Northern Territory. A lot of wild Brumby can be found living in the Australian Alps and in national parks. Life is tough for Australia's feral horse population, faced with poisonous plants and dingoes as predators. Many believe that Brumbies are damaging the environment, but nonetheless the state government has made a decision to protect the species.

Health check

Keeping your horse in good health is vital. Daily checks mean that you have a better chance of spotting something before it gets too bad to fix. Here are some handy hints about what to look out for!

> Your horse should be alert—ears pricked up or flicked forward and back

> Coats should be shiny and smooth, not greasy

> Weeping eyes or nose are not a good sign, so get those checked

> Loss of appetite could indicate illness

> Rearing or bolting when being ridden could actually be a sign of dental problems!

 Always speak to your vet as soon as you spot anything worrying. It's better to be safe than sorry!

Vaccinations

Keep your horse up to date with all of its vaccines. They protect your pet from harmful diseases.

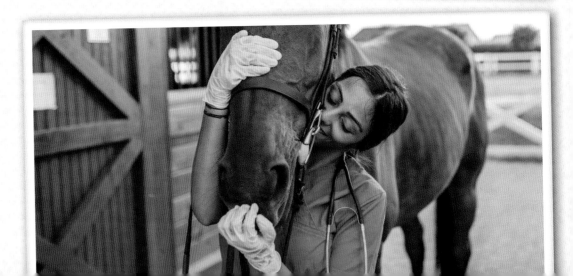

Eye care

Bathing your horse's eyes and nose in clean water using a sponge should be part of your horse's regular check-ups. Always change the water when you switch between cleaning its eyes and nose!

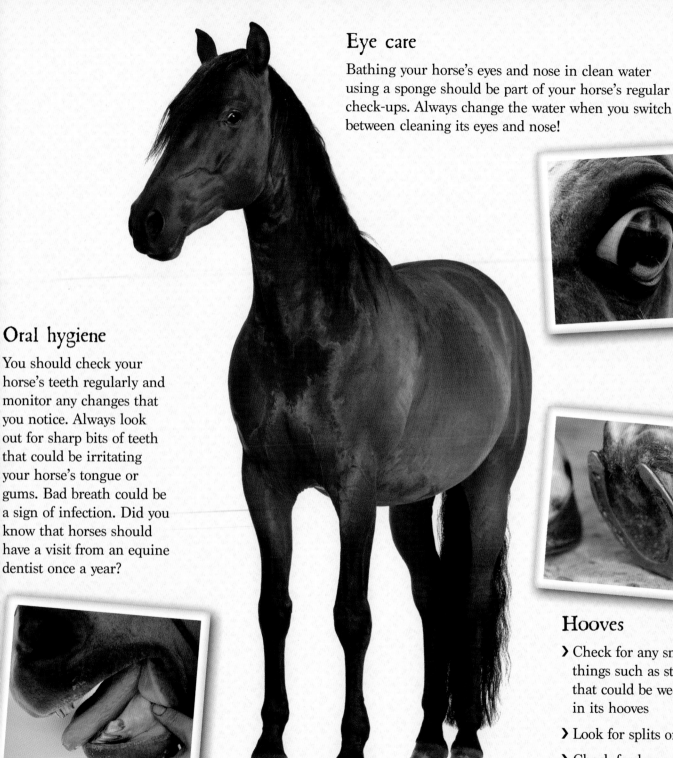

Oral hygiene

You should check your horse's teeth regularly and monitor any changes that you notice. Always look out for sharp bits of teeth that could be irritating your horse's tongue or gums. Bad breath could be a sign of infection. Did you know that horses should have a visit from an equine dentist once a year?

Hooves

> Check for any small things such as stones that could be wedged in its hooves

> Look for splits or cracks

> Check for loose shoes

Dream diet

Unsurprisingly, diet is a very important factor in ensuring a healthy, happy horse. Here are some dos and don'ts when it comes to feeding time.

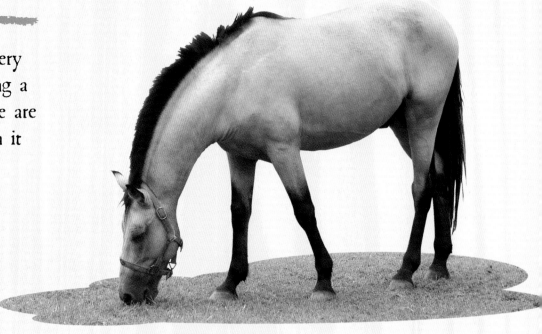

Fresh water

Ideally horses need a 24-hour supply of fresh water and grass to graze on.

Fruit

Too much fruit can be bad for your horse. Little amounts should be given as treats.

Get advice from a vet to make sure that you feed your horse the right amount of each food type. Horses might need additional types of food to maintain the right bodyweight.

Good

Apple

Banana

Carrot

Celery

Cow parsley

Grass

Hay

Mint leaf

DIY horse treats
Here are three plants that you can grow yourself.

Cow parsley

Throw seeds into shady soil. It flowers from April to June and is likely to spread quite far! Cow parsley helps with horse digestion.

Nettles

If you have nettles, try snipping them and letting them wilt to lose their sting. Nettles provide horses with plenty of iron.

Mint

Growing a mint plant at home means that you have a ready supply from Spring through to Fall. Be sure to pick the leaves often.

Poisonous

Lots of plants are dangerous to horses, so make sure that all are completely removed from any areas that your horse has access to.

Buttercups **Foxglove**

Deadly nightshade

Bad

Chocolate

Garlic

Meat

Onion

Potato

Tomato

Moldy or dusty hay

Grooming your pony

Grooming keeps your pony clean and healthy. It is your chance to check that your pony is in tip-top condition. Ponies love being groomed, so it is a great way to pamper your pony and to form a lasting friendship. The best time to groom is before and after you've taken your pony out for a ride.

Essential grooming equipment

To groom your pony you need a few basic tools. Every pony needs its own personal grooming kit. That way it reduces the chance that any parasites or germs will get passed from one pony to another. Make sure you keep your kit clean. Check out these essential grooming tools:

Dandy brush

Metal curry comb

Plastic curry comb

Horse sponge

Mane comb

Body brush

Cleaning the feet

A day of fun outside can leave your pony with mud and stones stuck in its shoes. You should carefully remove those using a hoof pick. This is known as "picking out." Keep an eye out for any problems or cuts while you are doing this.

Sponge the muzzle

Use a damp sponge to give your pony a face wash. Clean the eyes and the eyelids. Then make sure the muzzle is clean by gently sponging down the nostrils and lips.

Brush the tail

Make sure you stand safely to one side of your pony before brushing its tail. Hold the tail in one hand and run your fingers through the tail to get rid of any twigs. Then use a soft body brush to brush out any tangles and knots. Never use a harder dandy brush or curry comb as they can damage the tail.

Did you know?

Your pony can't tell you if it's in pain the way a person can. Keep a look out for any scratches or problems while grooming, such as limping or a lack of interest in food.

Brushing the coat and mane

Remove any dried mud from your pony's coat with a rubber curry comb or a dandy brush. Besides cleaning its coat, brushing improves your pony's circulation, plus it gets rid of dead skin and parasites that could cause infection.

Lipizzan

Stylized jumpers

The Lipizzan, or Lipizzaner, is a breed
of horse originating from Lipica in
Slovenia and was developed for royalty.
They wanted a horse that would be
a prize-winner at shows, as well as
suitable to work in the army. These
striking gray-white creatures are
usually born dark, then lighten as they
get older. Lipizzan are smart horses
that learn quickly, and they're known
for their ability to pull off stylized
jumps and precision moves.

Dressage and jumping

For some horse lovers, competing in dressage and jumping events is the best part of riding. You've probably heard of these events, but how much do you actually know about them?

Dressage: the basics

Dressage is a skilled and competitive form of riding. It has been an Olympic sport since 1900. You can compete at many levels, but higher levels require lots of practice, so riders and their horse partners have to be willing to put in lots of hours of training.

Interested in taking part in dressage? Here are some tips on where to start:

1. Before training for dressage a rider must have a strong bond with their horse, so spend plenty of time with them to build up trust.

2. To stay safe, you'll need a dressage saddle, saddle liner, stirrups, bridle, and reigns.

3. Riders must be healthy and fit—most train for 3 to 5 days a week.

4. Having professional training is a good idea. Trainers can teach you the technical elements and help you with whatever you find tricky.

Did you know?
Dressage is a French term that means "training."

Jumping: the basics

Show jumping events can be either indoor or outdoor. Horses and ponies must run around a course of colorful fences without knocking them down—you get a fault if that happens! Whoever has the fastest time with the least faults wins.

Want to get involved in jumping? Here are some pointers:

1. Jumping can be dangerous, so you need the right equipment to stay safe. Those include a safety approved helmet, boots, and a saddle that's suitable for jumping (not a dressage one!).

2. Be sure that you have mastered your walk, trot, and canter before trying to jump.

3. Find a professional teacher. They will make sure that you train in a safe environment. Only practice when you are with someone who can watch!

4. Your horse needs to be calm and relaxed before attempting any jumps.

Jump for joy!

Jumping can and should be fun, but it is important to get advice from professionals. They can give you guidance on equipment, clothing, and other safety tips.

Marwari

Courageous creatures

This rare breed is from the Marwar region of India, but it is loved around the globe. Unlike your average horse, the Marwari's ear tips turn inward. Some Marwari horses are only 14 hands high. These horses were favored during World War I for their courage and endurance. Fortunately, today they are more likely to be found at show jumping events! Marwari come in lots of colors from chestnut to pinto, but were originally black.

Thoroughbred

The stars of horse racing!

The Thoroughbred is a specific breed of horse that is famous for its speed and determination. They were developed in Britain for racing and jumping in the 17th century. They're very athletic, which helps to make them incredibly speedy. Thoroughbreds take part in many competitions besides racing, including dressage and show-jumping events.

THOROUGHBREDS ARE SOME OF THE **FASTEST** ANIMALS IN THE WORLD!

Racing

Horse racing is one of the most-watched and loved sports in the world. These events bring together some of the best horses to race on a variety of courses from flat racing to jumps.

Types of races:

> Flat racing—an event happening on a level racecourse

> Steeplechase—racing around a course with obstacles including fences and ditches

> Harness racing—horses must run at a specific gait and often pull a two-wheeled cart with a driver

> Endurance riding—long distance races that can be any length

> Maiden racing—contests for horses that haven't won a race before

Riders in races are called jockeys. There is no height limit, but jockeys are usually quite short and light. Before a race, jockeys must be weighed. Lead weights must be added if they're too light!

HORSES CAN RUN AT A SPEED OF **40MPH**

Famous racing events:

› Kentucky Derby (USA)
› The Grand National (UK)
› Royal Ascot (UK)
› Melbourne Cup (Australia)

Horses often race until they are around 12 years old. The oldest winning racehorse was 19 years old!

Racetracks are made from dirt, turf, or a synthetic surface that is suitable for horses.

Did you know?

England's King, Henry VIII, loved horse racing. So does Queen Elizabeth II!

ALL RACEHORSES SHARE AN OFFICIAL BIRTHDAY ON JANUARY 1ST

Palio di Siena

The Palio di Siena is Italy's most famous horse race. It's held twice every year on July 2nd and August 16th. Thousands of people come to Piazza del Campo to watch the race, which only lasts around 90 seconds. The jockeys famously ride bareback at the event that began in medieval times.

UNLIKE MOST HORSE RACES, IT IS THE HORSE AND NOT THE RIDER WHO **WINS!**

BEFORE RACING, HORSES ARE BLESSED AT CHURCH

Rodeo and Polo

You've probably heard the names of these popular equestrian sports, but how much do you really know about them?

Fast facts: Rodeo

> Competitive, multi-event individual sport

> Originated from cattle herding in Spain and Mexico

> It began as a game between cowboys, and in the 1800s it became an organized event

> To catch cattle, cowboys needed to be skilled with a rope and a lasso

> Today riders display their cowboy tricks and skills, e.g. saddle bronc riding and barrel racing

> There are two event categories— rough stock and timed events

THE NAME "RODEO" COMES FROM THE SPANISH WORD "RODEAR," THIS MEANS "TO ENCIRCLE"

THE NAME "POLO"
COMES FROM THE
INDIAN WORD "PULU,"
WHICH WAS THE NAME
OF THE WOODEN BALL

Fast facts: Polo

› One of the world's oldest equestrian sports

› It began in Central Asia

› Competitive team sport

› Two teams of four players

› Can be played on a field outdoors,
   or in an arena indoors

› A polo field is 300 yards long and 160 yards
   wide, and goal posts are eight yards apart

› Each match has four plays and each of them
   last seven minutes

› The aim is to drive a wooden ball down the
   field and into the goal using a mallet

Horses through history

Our four-legged friends have done so much for human beings throughout history. They've stood by us while we fought wars, mined deep underground, and plowed fields—not to mention how they've brought us joy as our beloved companions.

The special bond and relationship between humans and horses goes back a long way. Evidence suggests that horses were domesticated around 6,000 years ago!

Transportation

Before cars or trains were invented, horses pulling carts or wagons were the transport of choice. After the invention of the steam engine, horses were used much less. Today, large horses such as Shires are a popular attraction at tourist spots and at festivals.

Mining

Known as mining horses, or pit ponies, these horses worked in dark, underground mines. Horses first started working underground in the 1700s. At one point there were 70 thousand registered pit ponies. Being so deep underground in pitch black mines was not pleasant—in fact it was pretty dangerous down there!

War horses

These loyal and reliable creatures played a crucial role in World War I (1914–18). This was an era when technology was rapidly developing, but it was so new that people still relied heavily on horses. They did everything from carrying soldiers into battle to moving and transporting essential supplies.

HORSES WERE ALSO USED IN WORLD WAR II TO TRANSPORT SOLDIERS AND CARRY MEDICAL **SUPPLIES**

Working horses

Horses that protect

The first mounted police officers began patrolling in London, UK in 1758. US police forces began using horses in the late 1800s. From public events to city parks, horses help officers fight crime and keep communities safe. Horses are useful in large crowds because they're so large. So, when police are riding them, they have a clear view over everyone. A lot of the breeds chosen as police horses come from Ireland and are large and athletic. They also help make the police visible to the public.

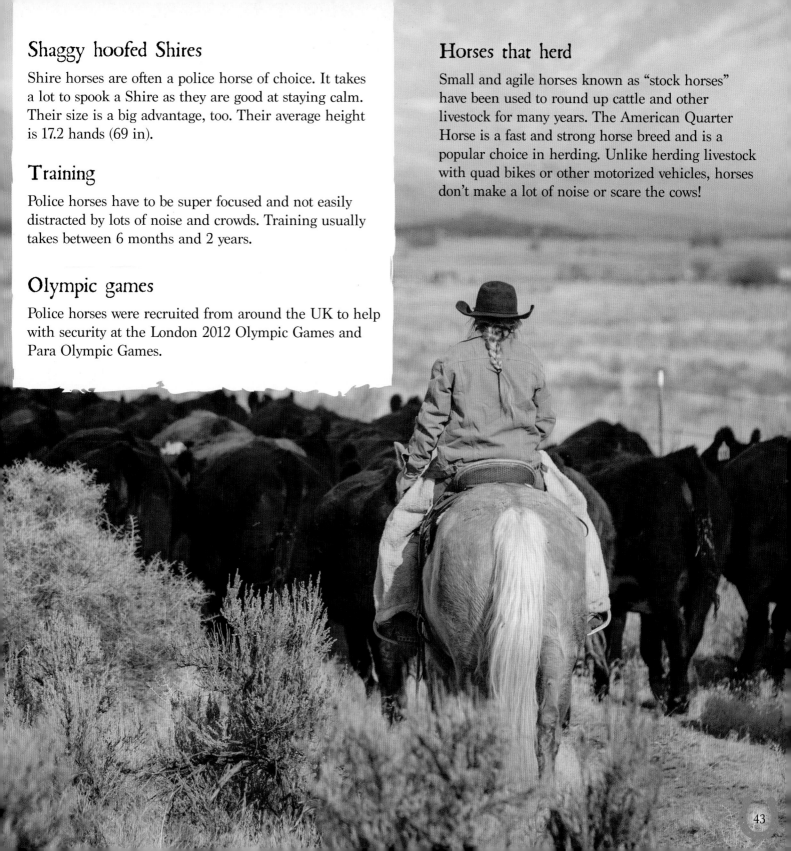

Shaggy hoofed Shires

Shire horses are often a police horse of choice. It takes a lot to spook a Shire as they are good at staying calm. Their size is a big advantage, too. Their average height is 17.2 hands (69 in).

Training

Police horses have to be super focused and not easily distracted by lots of noise and crowds. Training usually takes between 6 months and 2 years.

Olympic games

Police horses were recruited from around the UK to help with security at the London 2012 Olympic Games and Para Olympic Games.

Horses that herd

Small and agile horses known as "stock horses" have been used to round up cattle and other livestock for many years. The American Quarter Horse is a fast and strong horse breed and is a popular choice in herding. Unlike herding livestock with quad bikes or other motorized vehicles, horses don't make a lot of noise or scare the cows!

Horses that heal

Being able to respond to human emotions and behavior make our equine friends the perfect choice for animal therapy.

The use of animals in therapy has been going on for thousands of years. Horses have a unique way of understanding and mirroring human emotion, making them good for mental health related therapy. These incredible creatures can even synchronize their heartbeat to ours!

DO YOU NEED **TO BE AN** EXPERIENCED HORSE RIDER? ABSOLUTELY NOT!

Why horses?

Horses are herd animals. This means that they are sociable and enjoy company. Making bonds is much easier with sociable animals! These creatures are also experts when it comes to reading body language. They can pick up on signals to help therapists understand the things that worry you.

How does it work?

Horse therapy involves a team including a horse, a therapist, and a horse expert. The team works with the patient and comes up with specific exercises and tasks to help guide them into recovery.

In a typical session, patients are encouraged to...

> interact with the horse

> try out exercises, such as leading the horse around without using a lead rope

> think about how the activities make them feel and share what they think worked well

> reflect on their behavior

> build a bond with the horse

Did you know?

Therapy can help with lots of different things, such as low self-confidence and anger.

45

Famous horses

Prepare to meet the horses who made history, from beloved literary characters to the record-breaking race champions who stunned the world!

THE MOVIE WAS NOMINATED FOR TWO GOLDEN GLOBES, **FIVE BAFTAS** AND SIX ACADEMY AWARDS

Joey, *War Horse*

Meet the star of the award-winning play, *War Horse*. The play is based on Michael Morpurgo's novel about a farm horse named Joey, who was bought by the British army. That meant that he had to leave behind his best buddy, Albert—a teenager who raised him on the farm. The book was written in 1982. The story has also been made into a movie directed by Steven Spielberg.

Black Beauty

This world-famous and best-selling book was written in 1877 by Anna Sewell. It's all about the life of a horse called Black Beauty. The author loved animals and relied on a horse after spraining her ankle as a child. The book teaches people about the importance of animal welfare and encourages everyone to treat all living things with respect.

Did you know?

People believe that *Black Beauty* was based on one of Anna's family pets.

Bucephalus

This strapping horse was owned by Alexander the Great. Named Bucephalus or Bucephalas, this creature was much loved. It is believed that Bucephalus died after the Battle of the Hydaspes in 326 BC in Pakistan. Today Bucephalus is undoubtedly one of the most famous horses in history.

Secretariat

An American Thoroughbred named Secretariat was an out-of-this-world racehorse. He is famous for becoming the first Triple Crown winner in 25 years when he won The Belmont Stakes by an impressive 31 lengths. The historical race took part in 1973 and is described as one of the greatest races of all time. Although other horses have gone on to win the Triple Crown, Secretariat's record-breaking result is unbeaten.

Fabulous foals

Baby horses are called foals from the day they are born until they're a year old. Learn about everything that happens to a foal during their first year in the world!

Get up

Foals are far from helpless when they're born. Within an hour, it is normal for a foal to stand up. Being able to get up and move around so quickly means that horses are safer in the wild because they can run from danger.

11 months

A mare is pregnant for around 11 months. Foals stay with their mother for between six months and a year.

Chomp!

Foals live off their mother's milk for many months. They begin trying to eat grass after about a week.

Long legs!

Foals are born with their legs almost full-size—they don't grow much after they're born.

FOALS ARE USUALLY BORN **AT NIGHT**

AFTER A HORSE IS ONE YEAR OLD IT IS CALLED A **YEARLING**

Mongolian horses and eagle hunters

Hunting with Golden Eagles on horseback is an age-old tradition. In Mongolia, you rarely see a human being without a horse. These creatures are a massive part of day-to-day life and the more a person has, the wealthier they are seen to be. They are hardy horses that can cope with extremes in temperature and live outdoors all year round.

Riding and gaits

Mastering your basic gaits is key to riding success! Plenty of patience and practice is all it takes.

Horse gaits are . . .

The different ways that horses move. These can either be natural movements, or ones that people teach or train them to do. Horses have five natural gaits:

> walk

> trot

> canter

> gallop

> back

Walk, trot and canter are the first three gaits that a rider should master. Do those well and everything else is sure to come easier! It's all about being confident with the changes in speed. Practice is super important as well as not expecting to get it right every time.

Did you know?

If you ever decide to show your horse in dressage competitions, you'll need to be able to prove your skills in these areas!

American Paint Horse

It's pretty easy to recognize these distinctive horses. They have bold white and dark markings in irregular shapes. American Paint Horses originate in the United States. Besides their beautiful markings, these horses are also gentle and smart, which makes them a popular choice in competitions and shows.

Peruvian Paso

The friendly and graceful Peruvian Paso breed is sometimes called the Peruvian Horse. They are muscular yet elegant and known for their four-beat gait (way of moving) called the "paso llano," which makes riding them comfortable and smooth. Their good temperament makes these creatures a popular choice for beginners since they are easy to work with.

Irish Draught

Meet the national horse breed of Ireland. The Irish Draught were originally bred for working on farms. Being athletic makes this breed great for jumping events and dressage. Their calm nature means that they cope well under pressure and are not easily stressed. These are the characteristics that make Irish Draughts a safe breed to be used as police horses.

Maremmano

This beautiful Italian breed comes from the Maremma region of Tuscany and Northern Lazio. Maremmano come in a wide variety of solid colors—the most common are black, bay, brown, gray, and chestnut. They are hard-working with an unusually good memory. Despite not being as speedy as some other breeds, the Maremmano are still used for horse riding.

Sorraia

Here are a few key facts about the ancient dun-colored Portuguese breed called Sorraia. Today the rare breed is mostly found in Portugal and Germany and is sometimes used for herding work. These hardy horses are adaptable as they can survive harsh climates and live off little food. Sorraia are versatile and easy-to-train creatures.

Knabstrupper

This rare Danish horse breed often has a distinctive spotted coat, similar to the Appaloosa. In fact, they share the same color gene, which is called the "Leopard complex."

Camargue horses

Horses of the sea

The beautiful gray—almost white—Camargue horses gallop through the coastal sea and rivers of the Rhône Delta in southern France. They live in the wetlands of the Camargue—an area of rivers, streams, lakes, and salt marshes where the River Rhône meets the sea. The horses are semi-wild and share the National Park with black bulls and pink flamingos. This ancient breed of horse has been roaming the area for thousands of years and is possibly descended from prehistoric horses.

Bull-herders

Camargue horses are small but very strong and hardy. They are bred by the cowboys of the Riviera, known as the guardians. The guardians preserve a traditional way of life and use the horses to herd the Camargue black bulls. At birth, the Camargue horses are a dark brown, their coat slowly becoming paler until it is almost white by the time they are five years old. Camargue horses have tough hooves and are very strong, but agile and intelligent.

Horses of the world

Take a moment to explore the rarest of horse breeds as we journey around the globe.

Akhal-Teke

National emblem

The striking Akhal-Teke is a horse breed from Turkmenistan in Central Asia. Today they are found living in Russia or Turkmenistan. It is estimated that the Akhal-Teke breed is about 3,000 years old! The breed has a reputation for being smart and speedy, too! Take a look at the metallic shine of their coats—it's no wonder that they've been nicknamed "Golden Horses."

AKHAL-TEKE ARE THE NATIONAL EMBLEM OF TURKMENISTAN

Ardennes

Ancient breed of Europe

This breed of draft horse has been named after the Ardennes area of Belgium, Luxembourg, and France. They are stocky horses with muscular legs, which helps them to cope with walking over rough terrain. Their calm personality makes these horses easy to work with.

Did you know?

They were the breed of choice for historical figures such as Napoleon and Julius Caesar.

Fell

Shiny show pony

These working ponies traditionally come from the mountains and moorlands of Cumberland and Northumberland in England. Fell ponies have tons of positive traits, including the fact that they can move quickly and easily. This is probably why they are excellent jumpers! As well as being agile, these ponies are tough and adaptable to different environments and climates, making them great at cross-country treks. Today, Fell ponies are popular for trekking, herding, and competitions.

American Cream

The gold champagne gene

This unique-looking breed of draft horse began in the US and still exists today—although it is very rare. American Creams have piercing amber eyes and a distinctive cream-colored coat, which is called "gold champagne." This color combination makes them difficult to miss. Of all the breeds of draft horse that were developed in the US, the American Cream is the only one that is still around.

Caspian

Spectacular and speedy

This little horse breed originates in Northern Iran. Despite being very small (their size varies between 9 and 11.2 hands), the Caspian is still a horse and not a pony. This is because its appearance and personality is more similar to horses. The most common Caspian colors are bay, gray, black, dun, and chestnut.

THEIR SMALL SIZE AND GENTLE NATURE MAKE CASPIAN HORSES POPULAR WITH CHILDREN AND ELDERLY RIDERS

Hackney

Ballerinas of the show ring

This athletic breed is called the Hackney. The breed was developed in the UK especially for driving carriages. Hackneys are admired for the elegant way they move, and for their high step when they walk. Many Hackneys are shown by their owners at harness events, which involve horses trotting while pulling a two-wheeled cart known as a "sulky."

Did you know?

Today you will see plenty of Hackneys taking part in dressage and other competitions.

Gauchos of Argentina

Gauchos are skilled horsemen and herders in Argentina's Pampas (the plains in South America). They choose to live simply, away from modern life.

Criollo horses are native to South America and are popular with Gauchos. These horses survive in extreme climates and they are known for their incredible stamina.

65

Pony pictures

We all love looking at pony pics, so here's a gorgeous gallery just for you! It features everything from Dales to the Shetland. Which is your favorite?

› **Chincoteague pony**
found in USA

› **Connemara pony**
found in Ireland, UK

› **Shetland pony** found in Scotland, UK

› Welsh mountain pony
found in Wales, UK

› Bosnian pony found in Bosnia

› Garrano pony
found in northern Portugal

› Esperia Pony found in Italy

Horse gallery

Feast your eyes on some
of our favorite horse breeds!

› Andalusian horse

found in Spain

› Morgan horse found in USA

› Belgian horse found in Belgium

› **Mongolian horse** found in Mongolia

› **Spotted Saddle horse** found in USA

› **Curly horse** found in USA

› **Russian Trotter horse** found in Russia

Glossary

Bareback
Riding without a saddle

Dressage
Skilled form of riding during competitions
and exhibitions

Equine
Horses or members of the horse family, such
as ponies

Foal
A young or baby horse

Gait
This describes the various ways that a horse can
move, e.g. canter or trot

Mare
Female horse

Paddock
Field or enclosure where horses are kept

Polo
Team sport involving players mounted
on horseback

Rodeo
Contest where cowboys showcase their skills,
such as riding broncos or barrel racing

Index